Hand Play

Written by Elspeth Graham
Photographs by Tim Platt

Collins

Hand shadow puppets are
fun and easy to do.
Get a desk lamp.
Point the lamp at
a plain background.
Switch it on.

desk lamp

Lift one hand up to the light. You will see a shadow on the background. Next try to make some shadow shapes.

shadow

Make a flying bat.
Cross hands like this.

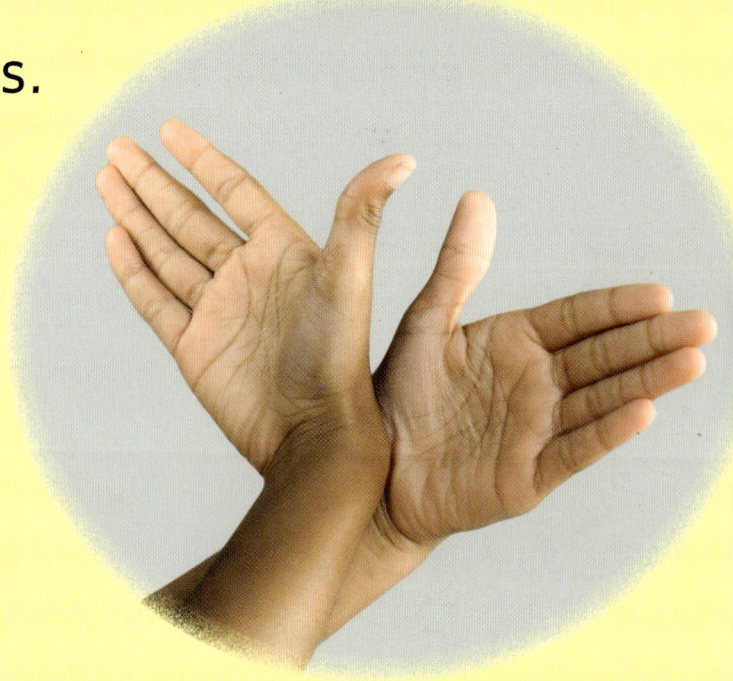

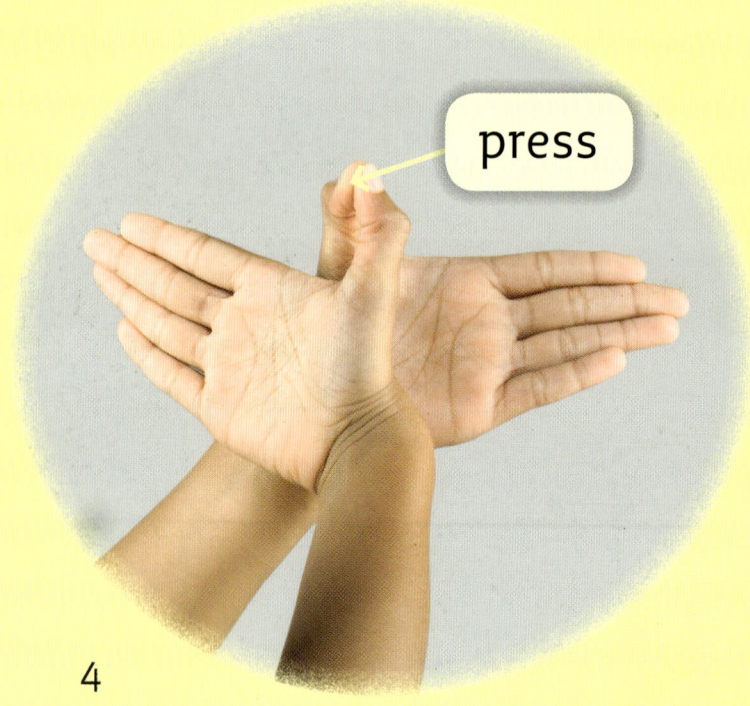

press

Then link hands
and press together.

Keep hands out flat to make the wings.
Make the fingers go up and down to make
the wings flap. Make the bat flap and swoop.

up and down

Next, make
a barking dog.
Reach out one
hand like this.

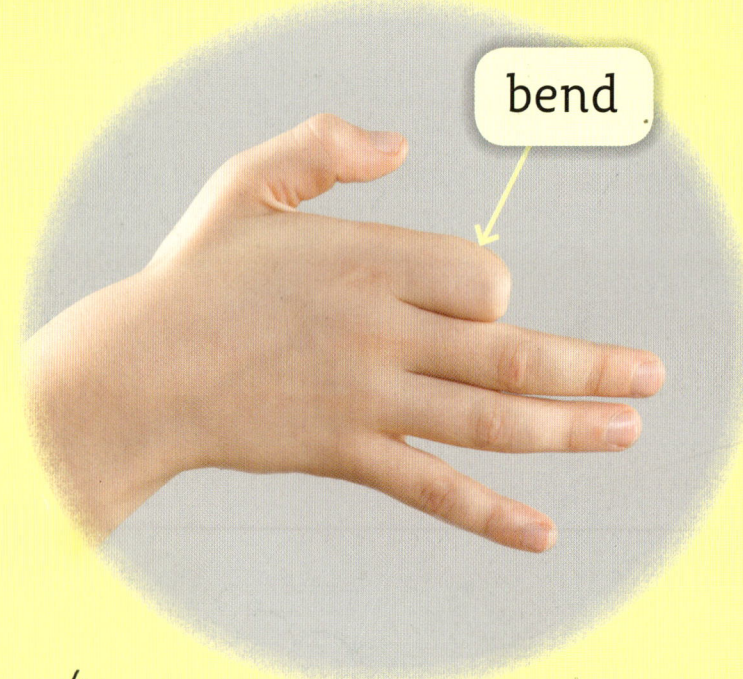

bend

Bend a finger back.

Make the little finger go up and down to make the dog bark. You can make the dog get a stick.

up and down

Make a duck.
Raise one arm.

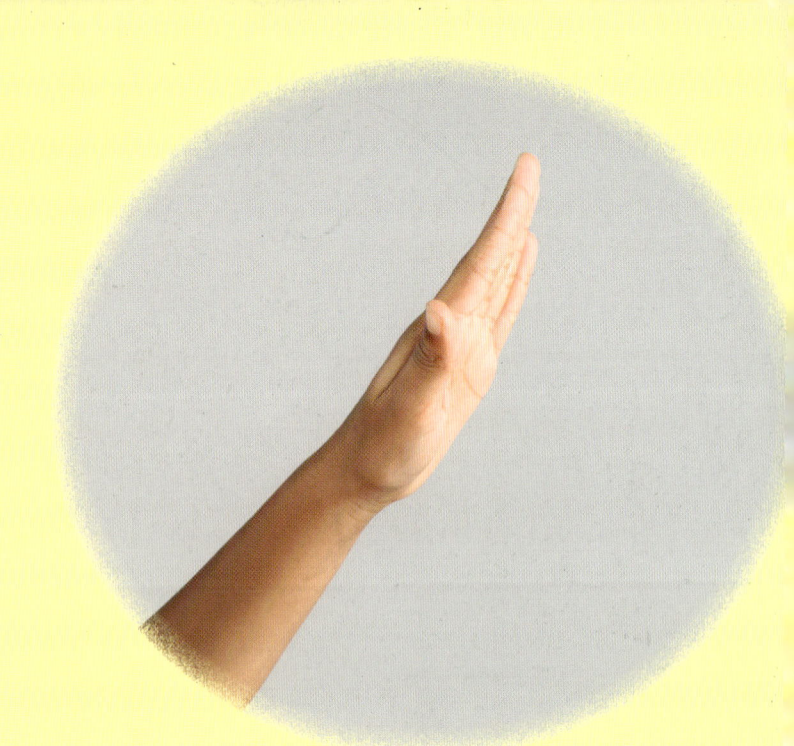

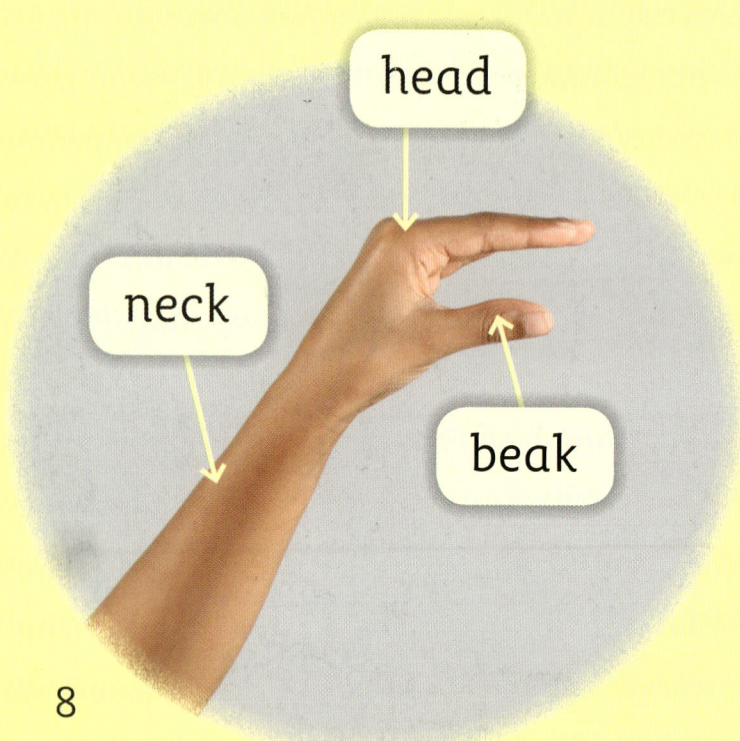

head

neck

beak

Bend the hand.
The arm is
the neck.
The fingers make
the beak.

bend

peck

Make the fingers go up and down as the duck pecks for grain. Bend the neck as it pecks.

Make a snail.
Make one hand flat.
Tuck the fingers
in tight.
This will make
the snail body.

finger for feeler

Lower a finger
to make a feeler.

Make the second hand into a fist. Sit the fist on the back of the flat hand. This makes the snail shell.

fist for shell

Make up a play for the hand shadows.
The dog can bark at the duck.

The duck can peck at the snail.

Think of shapes to make. Try to make a cat or a rabbit or a crab. Have fun!

Shadow puppets

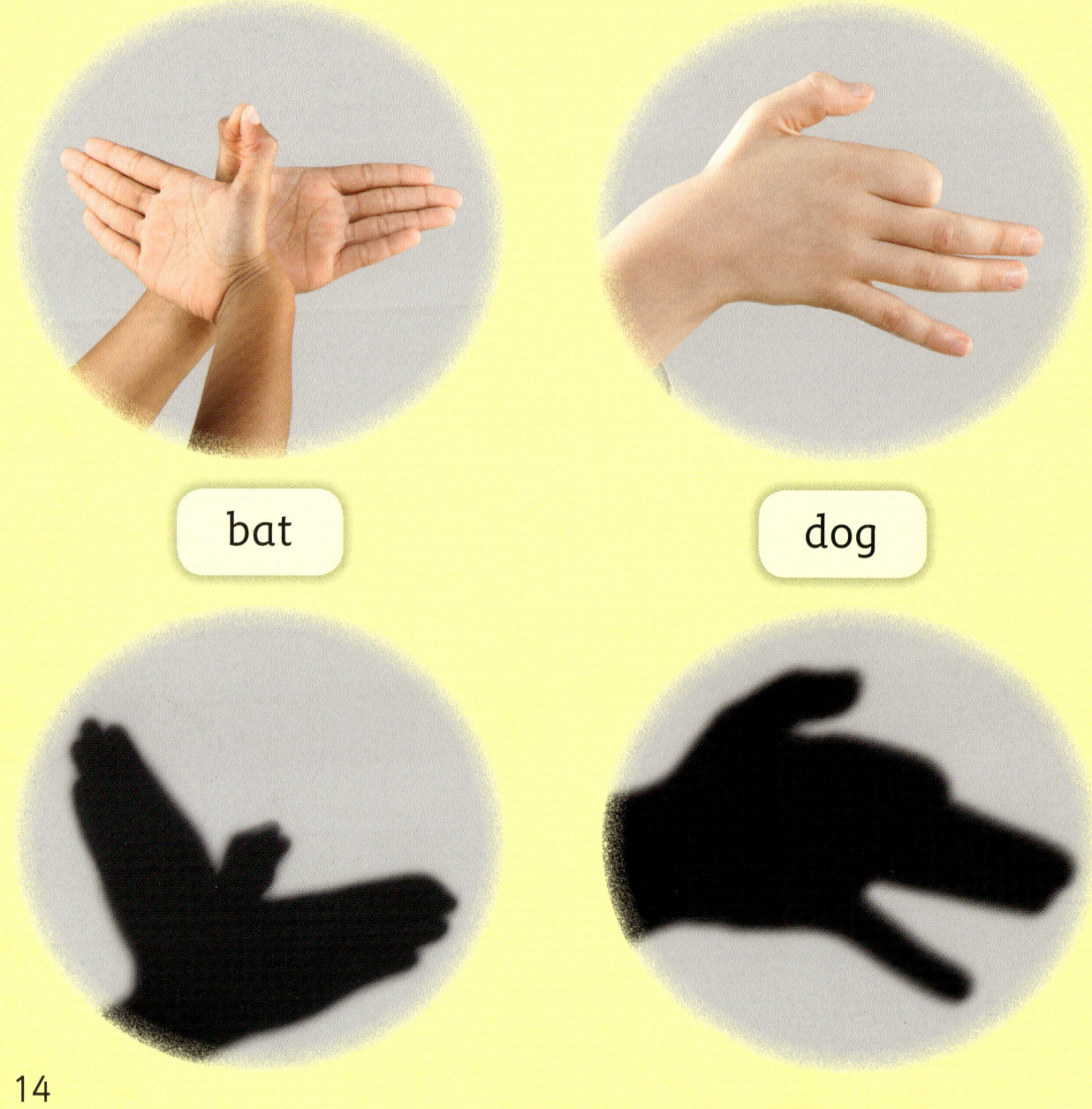

bat

dog

14

duck

snail

15

Ideas for reading

Written by Linda Pagett B.Ed(Hons), M.Ed
Lecturer and Educational Consultant

Learning objectives: apply phonic knowledge and skills as the prime approach to reading and spelling unfamiliar words that are not completely decodable; recognise automatically an increasing number of familiar high frequency words; recognise the main elements that shape different texts; distinguish fiction and non-fiction texts; recognise and use alternative ways of pronouncing graphemes already taught

Curriculum links: Science

Focus phonemes: ay, a-e, ea (reach), y, igh (tight), ow

Fast words: little, do

Word count: 258

Getting started

- Use flash cards to revise the focus phonemes with children.
- Read the title together. Ask children if they can guess what hand play means. Encourage them to use the pictures to help them, e.g. *What do you think these children might be doing? What characters might the shadows be?*
- Read the blurb on the back cover. Point out that it is an instruction book and discuss what this means. Practise giving each other simple instructions such as *Stand up*, and discuss where we find instruction texts, e.g. recipe books.
- Use magnetic letters to make the word *play* and add sound buttons and lines to it. Ask children to think of other words that contain the phoneme *ay*, e.g. may, pay, day.

Reading and responding

- Demonstrate how to read pp2–5 and follow instructions.
- Dwell on longer two-syllable and three-syllable words and model how to use phonic knowledge and strategies, as well as word knowledge to read them.
- Encourage children to read to p13 independently, taking time to look at the pictures and using decoding skills to help read and make meaning.